THE SIMPLE GUIDE TO

NEPAL

CUSTOMS & ETIQUETTE

COVER ILLUSTRATION

Heavily-laden porter on the Himalayan peak of Tengboche, Nepal.

Photo F. Wing. Courtesy Image Bank

ABOUT THE AUTHOR

SUNIL KUMAR JHA was born in Saptari, Nepal, in 1944, and is a distinguished linguist. He took his BA and MA degrees at Tribhuvan University – the oldest and most reputed university in Nepal – in English language and literature. Later, on a British Council scholarship, he completed his further studies in phonetics and phonology at the University of Essex where he received his PhD. Dr Jha is Professor of English at Tribhuvan University, Nepal.

ILLUSTRATED BY
IRENE SANDERSON

THE SIMPLE GUIDE TO

NEPAL

CUSTOMS & ETIQUETTE

Sunil Kumar Jha

GLOBAL BOOKS LTD

Simple Guides • Series 1
CUSTOMS & ETIQUETTE

The Simple Guide to
NEPAL
CUSTOMS & ETIQUETTE

First published 1998 by
Global Books Ltd
PO Box 219, Folkestone, Kent CT20 3LZ, England

© Global Books Ltd 1998

ISBN 1–86034–095–4

British Library Cataloguing in Publication Data
A CIP catalogue entry for this book
is available from the British Library.

Set in Futura 11 on 12 pt by Bookman, Hayes, Middx
Printed and bound in Malta by Interprint Ltd

Contents

COUNTRIES IN THIS SERIES

MAP OF NEPAL

Foreword

Everest

As the last Hindu Kingdom and birthplace of the Buddha, Nepal has so much to offer. It has an extremely rich cultural heritage, encompassing a wide variety of ethnic groups and their colourful festivals, and it has the snow-covered 'thrones of the gods' – the Himalayas – which are one of Nature's most spectacular treasures. These wonderful features alone will make your trip to this Himalayan Kingdom truly fascinating and memorable.

The Nepalese people have rules of etiquette and pursue a way of life similar to those of their neighbours living in the Indian sub-continent, albeit with a local flavour, and what follows is a modest attempt to familiarize you with present-day Nepal and the Nepalese way of socializing. An understanding of the basic rules which govern social exchanges in Nepal, as well as some historical background and an introduction to the natural environment, will help you to get the most out of your visit to this country.

You will find that things are done here in more than one way, so when in Nepal, try to do as the Nepalese do: enjoy the mountains and the countryside; enjoy the sight of its stunning snowy peaks, as well as the rich variety of animal and plant life; enjoy the ancient royal cities of the Kathmandu Valley with its pagodas and palaces, the culture, the festivals, the food, as well as its popular music. There is nothing quite like it anywhere else in the world. And that includes the Nepalese welcome and hospitality.

SUNIL KUMAR JHA
Spring 1998

1

Introducing Nepal

Bicycle rickshaws, Kathmandu

It is, perhaps, Nepal's unique landscape, its cultural diversity, but above all its unforgettable people which make it such a remarkable country. Yes, it is among the ten poorest nations in the world but the Nepalese enjoy their lives, and nowhere else will you see so many smiling people as in Nepal.

Hinduism and Buddhism are united in Nepal in an almost inseparable unit, and provide a unique diversity of festivals and rituals. The *puja* in a monastery, the *bhajan* and *arti* in a temple, the little sacrifice on a household altar, the countless *thangkas* in the souvenir shops of Kathmandu – all these make a trip to Nepal so fascinating.

Visitors to Nepal should be aware of a unique feature of the country's history: it was never colonized by any Western country. This absence of a colonial past is important to an understanding of the Nepalese mentality. Since the Nepalese have no historic chips on their shoulders, visitors are welcomed here as equals. Racial and religious prejudice is virtually unknown. Nevertheless, over the centuries the people did do battle with their neighbours as well as local (indigenous) principalities. To know the country properly, therefore, it is essential to know the early, medieval and modern periods in Nepali history.

300 YEARS OF HISTORY

The Kingdom of Nepal, as we know it today, came into existence in 1769 when Prithvi Narayan Shah, the king of the small principality of Gorkha, successfully annexed several other principalities scattered to the east and west. Since the Kathmandu Valley, which was then known as the Nepal Valley, became the seat of power following unification, the new country gradually came to be known as Nepal.

Ever since unification, Nepal has been ruled by the preemptory and peremptory command (*Hukmi Sashan*) of the Shah Kings. The successors of King Prithvi Narayan Shah carried out their expansionist policies which led to wars – first, with Tibet in 1793, and then with the British in the south in 1814. The latter war ended with a treaty signed at Sugauli in 1818 in which Nepal lost almost two-thirds of its territory which, of course, had been acquired earlier through the process of expansion.

The loss of Nepalese territory heightened the intra-elite conflict and a bloody coup occurred in September 1846 in which an army general, named Jung Bahadur Rana, seized control and instituted the system of hereditary prime minister-ship in which the eldest male member of the Rana family alone could enjoy the position of Prime Minister. The Rana family rule continued in Nepal for 104 years until it was toppled by a minor revolution in 1950-51.

The political change of 1951 came as a result of the compromise reached between the then King, the Ranas, and the leaders of the Nepali Congress in New Delhi which was arranged by the then Indian Prime Minister Jawahar Lal Nehru. The compromise reduced the political power of the Ranas and restored the royal power and preroga-tives once again.

The introduction of a democratic political system in Nepal proved a formidable task. The first popular government of the Nepali Congress was dismissed on 15 December 1960. For the next 30 years a party-less Panchayat system, introduced by King Mahendra and continued with refinements by King Birendra, was tried in Nepal.

THE PRESENT POLITICAL SYSTEM

After King Mahendra's death in December 1971, his son Crown Prince Birendra succeeded to the throne as the King of Nepal. Finally, in April 1990 the 30-year-old party-less Panchayati rule in Nepal came to an end. The new constitution defines the multi-party system, constitutional monarchy and popular sovereignty as the fundamental features of the new polity. The constitution provides for a parliament consisting of two houses: the Lower House (*Pratinidhi Sabha*) and the Upper House (*Rastriya Sabha*).

The new constitution settled for a 'first-past-the-post' system to elect 205 members of the Lower House, while the single-transferable vote system was introduced to elect 50 members of the Upper House, which consists of 60 members including 10 royal nominees. The new constitution also lowered the voting age to 18 years from the earlier 21 years. The events of recent years clearly show that Nepal has accepted parliamentary democracy not only in principle but also in practice.

SOMETHING ABOUT THE GURKHAS

Today the holy castle of Gorakhnath watches over the city of Gorkha, to which the Gurkhas owe their name. The expression Gurkha or Gorkha has its origins in the Sanskrit words 'go' which in translation means 'cow'; and 'rakh' (raksha) which means 'protector'. An allusion is thus made to Hindu tradition as 'protector of the cows'.

Nepal earns some thirty million dollars a year as a result of the existence and activities of the Gurkhas. Besides tourism, they represent one of the most important sources of foreign exchange in this country.

The national weapon of Nepal, which is also the favourite weapon of the Gurkha soldiers, is the khukuri, a curved knife. No household in Nepal lacks one, where it is used to chop wood, meat and vegetables. The good luck of the Gurkha battalions is thought to depend on the aptitude of the Gurkha in the employment of his khukuri. As the symbol of the Gurkha army, crossed khukuris are illustrated in the Nepalese coat-of-arms.

Nepalese coat-of-arms featuring a mountain scene at the foot of the Hiamalayas with a cow (national animal), a pheasant (national bird) and rhododendrons (national flower) flanked by two Gurkha soldiers

Hindu with garlanded holy cow at the Gai Timar festival

2

The Natural Environment

Yaks carrying loads at high altitude

On entering the Kingdom of Nepal, the visitor finds himself in a region of incomparable orographic,* botanical, zoological and ethnic diversity. The kingdom lies along the southern slopes of the Himalayan mountain ranges. It is located between India to the east, south and west, and the Tibetan Autonomous Region of China to

---

* Orography is the study of mountains

the north. Its territory has an area of 54,718 square miles and it extends roughly 500 miles from east to west and 90 to 150 miles from north to south.

From south to north, Nepal can be divided into four main physical belts, each of which extends east to west across the country: first, the Tarai – a low, flat, fertile land adjacent to the border of India; second, the forested Churia foothills and the Inner Tarai Zone, rising from the Tarai plain to rugged Mahābhārat Lekh range; third, the mid-mountain region between the Mahābhārat Lekh range and the great Himalayas; and fourth, the great Himalaya range, rising to more than 29,000 feet (8,000 metres).

The geography of the country has led to the development of very clearly distinguished landscapes and natural regions. Drawn along the Indian border, Tarai is a lowland which forms the northern extension of the Gangetic Plain and varies in width from less than 16 to more than 20 miles. Known as the kingdom's bread-basket, the Tarai now yields some 77 per cent of the rice, 80 per cent of the oil-seed, 94 per cent of the sugar beet, and 94 per cent of the tobacco harvests. On account of the deforestation in recent years, Tarai today possesses only 10 per cent of Nepalese forest assets, but has 42 per cent of the agricultural lands.

Also situated in the Tarai is the main industrial area outside the Kathmandu Valley. Along-side the old sugar, cigarette and match factories, new cement factories, metal works, and other industries are being established. The Tarai comprises 23 per cent of the total land area of Nepal, and approximately 44 per cent of the Nepalese population lives here. Characteristic of this subtropical zone is its moist, warm climate with temperatures of over 40° centigrade in June/July.

Buddha's birthplace, called Lumbini, is situated in the Tarai, and it has become a famous place of pilgrimage for Buddhists from around the world. In 1967 the General Secretary of the United Nations, U. Thant – himself a pious Buddhist – visited Lumbini. At his initiative, a design was put forward for a programme of international support for the rebuilding and expansion of this pilgrimage destination. The Maya Devi Shrine, located nearby, was named after Siddhartha Buddha's mother, and located south of the shrine is the Pushkarni Pond, where Buddha is said to have taken his first purifying bath.

At the Siwaliks, which reach heights of around 4,400 feet (1,500 metres), one enters the foothills of the Himalayas. The land here is composed of a very unstable mixture of soft and hard rocks, gravel and sand, highly susceptible to erosion. The area cannot be used for agriculture, and is therefore barely inhabited. These forest-covered ranges are broken up by the gravelly beds of larger and smaller Himalayan rivers.

Those parts of the Tarai which are enclosed by the Siwalik hills and the Ganges plain, and which form shallow basins, are referred to as Tarai's interior or Inner Tarai. The eastern Rapti Valley, which also contains the Chitwan National Park, the Dang Valley, and the valleys of Sindhuli and Udaypur are all in Inner Tarai. Besides birds and butterflies, there are also many large mammals to be found in Inner Tarai such as elephants, the Indian rhinoceros, Bengali tigers, wild cattle, and various kinds of deer and apes.

The Mahābhārat chain is the pre-Himalayan mountain range which runs north of the Siwaliks over the entire length of the country. Its peaks range in height from between 6,500 and 10,000 feet (2,000 and 3,000 metres). With them we enter into an old Nepalese settlement area, which is protected from the south by fever-swamps, and from the north by the main range of the Himalayas. It is in this area that we find the valleys of Kathmandu and Pokhara with significant urban settlements.

The Kathmandu Valley, the political and cultural hub of the nation, is drained by the Bagmati River; the Pokhara Valley, 96 miles west of Kathmandu, is drained by the Seti River. The crops cultivated here include rice up to about 6,500 feet (2,000 metres), millet up to 7,700 feet (2,350 metres), corn – the main crop of the highlands – up to 8,200 feet (2,500 metres), and wheat up to 9,200 feet (2,800 metres). Around the attractive farmsteads one also finds fruit trees, and growing in their gardens are both leaf and root vegetables.

The main range of the Himalayas rises rather abruptly out of the highlands. Above the snow line, which is on average around 17,000 feet (5,200 metres) in altitude, the peaks are covered with permanent snowfields. The glaciers, which are resupplied with snow during the monsoons, feed the larger rivers. Eight of the ten highest peaks in the world are in this region, each of which exceeds 26,000 feet (8,000 metres) in altitude.

The eight-thousanders from west to east are: Dhaulagiri 26,794 feet (8,167m), Annapurna 26,545 feet (8,091m), Manaslu 26,758 feet (8,156m), Cho Oyu 26,748 feet (8,153m), Mt Everest 29,028 feet (8,848m), Lhotse 26,414 feet (8,051m), Makalu 27,805 feet (8,474m) and Kanchenjunga 28,208 feet (8,598m). The high mountains have only a few habitable places, and these are only sparsely populated. The Sherpas are the most well-known folk here.

The Himalayas play a significant role as a climate boundary. They separate the monsoon wet-lands to their south from the dry continental climate of the Tibetan plateau. The primary vegetation of the high mountains – juniper, rhododendrons and birches – is reduced to grasses and bushes, and low-growing, often thorny spices. The animal world includes mountain goats, yaks, foxes, wolves and rabbits.

The major rivers of Nepal are three: the Koshi, the Gandaki and the Karnali. The watershed of these rivers lies not along the line of the highest peaks in the Himalayas but to the north of it, usually in Tibet. In the upper courses of all Nepalese rivers, which run through mountain regions, there are little or no flood problems. In the low-lying areas of the Tarai plain, however, floods are a serious problem.

Top Tip: Watch the Altitude!

Nepal's climate, influenced by elevation as well as by its location in a sub-tropical latitude, ranges from sub-tropical monsoon conditions in the Tarai, through a warm temperate climate between 4,000 to 7,000 feet in the mid-mountain region, to cool temperate conditions in the higher parts of mountains between 7,000 (2133m) and 11,000 feet (3352m), to an Alpine climate at altitudes between 14,000 (4267m) and 16,000 feet (5832m) along the lower slopes of the Himalayas. At altitudes above 16,000 feet the temperature is always below freezing and the surface is always covered by snow and ice.

Among the animal species found in the Alpine zone are the musk deer, much persecuted for the musk pods they carry, the tahr, the goral, and wild sheep, which are preyed upon by wolves and snow leopards. Pheasant (the national bird of Nepal) are common.

Thus, the Kingdom of Nepal, now the home of 19 million people of various cultures, is a place with a wealth of life-forms and species; a landscape unequalled in its variety and beauty. The best time to travel in Nepal starts at the beginning of October and lasts until the end of April. May is relatively hazy and hot. The monsoon season lasts from the beginning of June to the end of September. During the autumn – from September to the end of November – in the central hill regions it is delightfully warm and also very comfortable in the evenings, but in the winter this region can be noticeably cool.

In the high-altitude tourist destinations weather conditions are often raw. The Tarai is therefore very suitable for a stay, whereas in summer it is the other way round. You get the clearest views from October to December, after which this period of beautiful weather is interrupted by a few days of persistent rain. The best time to go trekking is during the months of October, November, March and April. From March on, you can see the natural environment in its full splendour.

Top Tip: On The Yeti Trail

The Yeti (or 'Abominable Snowman') is said by the Sherpas to inhabit the high snow mountains of Nepal but has eluded discovery by several expeditions that have set out to solve the mystery of this fable. Strange tracks are often found in the snow, but opinion inclines to the belief that they are probably made by bears.

3

The People & Their Languages

A young Rai woman

THE PEOPLE

Most visitors to Nepal, especially those from the West, perceive this country as 'the Himalayan Kingdom of courteous people in the east'. This epithet says something about the Nepalese's traditional esteem for decorum, courtesy and propriety. You will find the Nepalese people warm, smiling, spontaneous, and informal –

four qualities that can be translated in one single Nepalese word: they are *milansar*. Indeed, the Nepalese are very friendly people, and their hospitality is internationally acclaimed.

Viewed historically, it was the large-scale migrations of Mongoloid groups of people from Tibet and Indo-Aryan people from northern India which accompanied the early settlement of Nepal. These groups of people have produced a diverse linguistic, ethnic, and religious pattern in Nepal.

The Nepalese of Indo-Aryan ancestry include the people of the Tarai, those of the hills, the Tharus, the Newars, and the Muslims – numbering nearly 80 per cent of Nepal's total population. Indo-Aryan ancestry has been a source of prestige in Nepal for centuries, and the ruling families have been of Indo-Aryan and Hindu background.

Top Tip: Respect for Monarchy & Temples

The Nepalese are intensely proud of their national heritage and Royal Family, therefore always show proper respect for the Nepalese monarchy. You are also expected to behave modestly and sensibly in all matters relating to the Hindu and Buddhist religions, especially when visiting temples. The temples of this Himalayan Kingdom are externally very photogenic, but please be careful when photographing inside temples in case there are restrictions. Remember to remove your shoes before entering a temple.

The Tibeto-Nepalese groups of people in Nepal include the Tamang, the Rai, the Limbu, the Bhote, the Sunwar, and so on. These groups live primarily in the north and east of Nepal. Some other Tibeto-Nepalese groups include the Magar and the Gurung, and they mostly inhabit west-central Nepal.

Nepal's northern border with Tibet is a high Himalayan country. Its valleys and mountain slopes are inhabited by Himalayan people who speak various Tibetan dialects and whose cultural and religious roots are Tibetan. The most famous among them are: the Sherpas, the Lhomis, the Manangbas, the Olangchung people, the Dolpo people, the Lopas of Mustang, and so forth.

The present literacy rate is about 40 per cent. According to the 1991 census, 90% of the nation's population is Hindu and eight per cent is Buddhist; the remainder belong to other religious faiths.

People living near the borders of the north and south have easy access to neighbouring countries for trade and social intercourse. The Mongoloid groups live primarily in the northern sections and adhere to Tibetan Buddhism and numerous 'natural religions'; the Indo-Nepalese groups live mostly in the southern half of the country, speak Indo-Aryan languages, and adhere to Hinduism as their religion.

Local woman and child from the spectacular Annapurna region

Both these border areas are within the sphere of influence of the respective neighbouring countries in matters of race, religion, language, culture and economy. But the middle regions of Nepal are far removed and rather isolated from such outside influence and culture. For this reason the middle hill people have always been strong nationalists and make some of the best soldiers in the world. A majority of Nepal's administrative officers come from this region. Mongoloid and Indo-Nepalese groups have contact with each other principally in this third main hill region of the country.

Most Nepalese live in the countryside. A typical rural family will include grandparents, cousins, an uncle or aunt, and even the children of distant relatives. Living together under one roof encourages natural courtesy, tolerance and mutual respect – all these strengthen the interests of social harmony. Even urban households retain these traditional values as far as their circumstances permit, and most of them keep and enjoy their links with the countryside.

Top Tip: Watch Out For The Main Course!

Should you be invited into a private home in Nepal or to some party, please keep in mind that the main course is traditionally served towards the end of the visit. Before that main course, the host offers you tasty little morsels such as fried liver, *sel roti*, a deep-fried rice-meal pastry, roasted chick peas and of course alcohol, if you happen to take it.

When grown up, sons and daughters usually go on living with their parents until they marry: married daughters normally go to their husbands' homes, but most married sons continue living with their parents.

Again, if youngsters choose to go for university-level studies, as a very high proportion do these days, they tend to live at home and attend the nearest college of Tribhuvan University – the oldest and most reputed university in Nepal spread in a nationwide complex. Such a supportive and protective upbringing seems to encourage self-confident and secure personalities.

From an early age, Nepalese people are brought up to accept a code of social behaviour based on respect for superiors, parents, teachers and the elderly. 'A guest in the house, God in the house' is a sentiment which is widely shared in Nepal.

> **Top Tip: Say Yes!**
>
> As hosts the Nepalese rarely take 'no' for an answer. You will be invited to try this or that dish even after you have said 'no thank you'. To avoid repeated urging to try the dish, you politely explain why it is that you cannot eat any more. If that does not work, try just a little bit and compliment the cook!

Nepalis tend to be quite direct and they more or less say what they think. They usually come straight to the point without much small talk. This may appear rude to some foreigners, but it is certainly not intended to be. This direct approach is adopted in a wide range of situations, from complaining about bad service to flattery or flirting.

Most Nepalese have three names: first, second, and surnames. First and second names are 'given names' or family names; surnames as such are based on the respective castes or social classes to which they belong. You may use the surnames of those who are completely unacquainted with you, but with Nepalis of even limited acquaintance it is quite acceptable to call them by their first names. On very formal occasions, however, you may use surnames, whether acquainted or unacquainted, with such honorific titles as Mr, Mrs, or Miss.

In the Nepalese countryside in particular, refrain from overtly expressing affection in public. Nobody minds a brief hug or kiss between you and your wife or girlfriend, especially at the bus station or airport, but you will attract attention if you do it repeatedly anywhere in public.

THE LANGUAGES

The 1991 Census Report lists 36 languages spoken in Nepal. Each one of these can be grouped in one of the following four language families: (1) Indo-European (Indo-Aryan Group), (2) Sino-Tibetan (Tibeto-Burman Group), (3) Austro-Asiatic (Munda Group), and (4) Dravidian (Northern Kudux Group). Of all these languages, only 12 are spoken by one or more than one per cent of the total population. These 12 'major' languages belong to just two language families – i.e. Indo-Aryan and Tibeto-Burman – as shown in Table 1.

Table 1: 12 Major Languages of Nepal

LANGUAGE FAMILY/ LANGUAGE	NO. OF SPEAKERS	% OF TOTAL POPULATION
A. Indo-Aryan		
1. Nepali	9302880	50.31
2. Maithili	2191900	11.85
3. Bhojpuri	1379717	7.46
4. Tharu	993388	5.37
5. Awadhi	374638	2.03
6. Hindi-Urdu	373205	2.02
B. Tibeto-Burman		
7. Tamang	904456	4.89
8. Newari	690007	3.73
9. Rai Group	439312	2.38
10. Magar	430264	2.33
11. Limbu	254088	1.37
12. Gurung	227918	1.23

Nepali is the main language of Nepal. It is also the officially sanctioned national language of the country and, although perhaps 80% all Nepalese can understand it, nearly half of the population speak other languages as their mother-tongues. Originally a language of the western hills, Nepali is now widely spoken in the Tarai, in the entire hill region, as well as in various other parts of the kingdom. It has a rich literature, and is used in education, mass media, administration, and also as a medium of wider communication throughout the country.

The second most widely spoken language in Nepal is Maithili. The main concentration of the speakers of this language lies in the Tarai regions as well as in the northern and eastern regions of the state of Bihar in India. Originally spoken in the ancient country of Mithila (Tirhut), Maithili has indeed been renowned from ancient times on account of its rich literature and traditions.

Bhojpuri and Awadhi are spoken mainly in the central and western Tarai regions. But the main concentration of the speakers of the Tharu language – which is essentially a hybrid language resembling Maithili, Bhojpuri, Awadhi and Magahi – lies in the inner Tarai regions as well as in the far-western Tarai regions of Nepal. Rajbanshi is spoken in the southern fringes of the Tarai extending from Morang to Jhapa districts. The speakers of Danuwar are found in the valley of Udaypur, Sindhuli and Makwanpur, as well as in the northern areas of Rautahat, Bara, Parsa and Chitwan districts.

The languages of the Tibeto-Burman group are spoken primarily in the Himalayan regions and in the mountain regions of Nepal. Tamang is spoken mainly along the Mahābhārat ranges around the Kathmandu Valley, whereas the main concentration of the speakers of Newari lies in the Kathmandu Valley itself. The Gurung and the Magar languages are spoken mainly in the central hill regions of Nepal.

Of the two main subdivisions of Kiranti, the Rai are the most numerous, inhabiting the traditional hill regions of Nepal. Rai settlements are mostly found at altitudes of three to six thousand feet above sea level – primarily spread along the valley slopes of the Dudh Koshi and Arun rivers and their tributaries.

The Limbu tribe is second in size to the Rai among Kirantis. Like their Rai cousins, the Limbu have an area of their own, traditionally called Pallo-Kirant. Limbuwan includes the area east of the Arun river extending to Nepal's eastern border with India's West Bengal. Tibetan is spoken along the entire east-west length of the Himalayan region punctuated by Sherpa, Lhomi and Thakali.

Limbu woman with traditional earrings

Everyday life in Kathmandu's New City

Social Occasions & Situations

Visitors to Nepal will find that the Nepalese are a very sociable people. Getting to know them is certainly worthwhile. But before doing so, visitors should try to learn something about their way of life and codes of behaviour.

GREETING AND *NAMASTE*

Nepalis greet each other very much in the same way as people do everywhere else in the world – i.e. with a cheery sign of recognition and a chat. The traditional Nepali greeting, and farewell, is to raise both hands gracefully, palm to palm and close to the body, in what is known as *namaste*. Though tempting, it would be a mistake to regard this as the equivalent of any handshake. In Nepal *namaste* means not only to greet and bid farewell; more importantly, it means to pay your respects to the recipient of it.

Namaste is accordingly always initiated by the person whose social status, for reasons of age or rank, is inferior to the person to whom respects are being paid. A person who initiates a *namaste* usually bends his head. The more you bend your head, the greater the respect you wish to convey. The recipient of a *namaste* normally, but not always, responds with a *namaste*. Watch the news on Nepal television and observe how people of different ages, rank and status say *namaste* and how the recipients respond. When the gap between the greeter and the recipient is quite significant, a *namaste* may be returned by its recipient only with a smile or a nod.

THE RAI PEOPLE

The Rais are a people of mongoloid stock living in the hills of eastern Nepal, north of the Mahābhārat range and south of the Himalayan range. The east-west extension of their area stretches between the Tamur and Rikhu rivers. The physical characteristics of the Rais include a broad, flat face and brown eyes, light-colour skin and black hair. The dress of the Rai females and their nose rings are very typical. On the whole, the Rais are well-mannered, cheerful and amicable people, characterized by a positive and open attitude towards life.

RELIGIONS

To understand why the Nepalese adore their deities and why they have continued to celebrate their numerous festivals down through the centuries, one must trace the religion which permeates every aspect of Nepalese life, culture and history. And to understand religion in Nepal, one must look both inside and outside her borders.

Officially, Nepal is the only Hindu kingdom in the world. That being so, Hinduism has been declared the national religion, but other religions are also tolerated. That is, there is no restriction on any other religions in Nepal. Here Hinduism and Buddhism have intermingled for centuries, and have interchanged ancient concepts of demons and ghosts established by Shamanism.

A Nepali, especially a Newar, can worship both Buddha and Shiva without falling into a conflict of beliefs. Frequently in rituals and religious festivals, especially in myths, the distinction between the gods is consciously blurred. The ancient *Nepala Mahatmya* texts say, 'To worship Buddha is to worship Shiva', the *Swayambhu Puran* reciprocates by recommending and sanctioning adulation of Lord Shiva.

Street scene in front of temple of Vishwanath & Krishna, Patan

Typically, a Nepalese pilgrim who visits a temple during a festival would strew his/her offerings – e.g. flowers, grains of rice, powdered cinnabar, coins, etc. – at all sorts of shrines and holy sanctuaries. At the main national holy sanctuary, Pashupatinath temple, hangs a sign, as at many other temples in Nepal, forbidding entrance to non-Hindus. However, since Buddha is considered in Hinduism to be a manifestation of Vishnu, Buddhists are allowed entrance.

M usic and dance are favourite pastimes among the Nepalese, not least because religious ceremonies require the use of drums and wind instruments that have been preserved from ancient times. Devotional songs are an important feature of most religious and family occasions; these songs have elements of both classical and folk music and have been used by some contemporary musical revivalists in their attempt to bridge the gap between the two.

RITUALS

I n Nepal most of the rituals surrounding the rites of passage (birth, coming of age, marriage and death) are usually limited to relatives.

T he birth of a child is an event which carries with it ritual impurification not only for the mother, but also for the entire house. It therefore requires particular purification rituals such as prayer, washing and dietary restrictions. A more cheerful ceremony is the first feeding of boiled rice to the baby at the age of about six months. This is a festive occasion and many relatives come together to celebrate the well-being of the world.

M arriage is the most elaborate ritual in which all relatives are invited. The marriage partner is generally chosen with reference to genealogy and caste-specific criteria. For the higher castes, or for people of high social status, a wedding is very expensive. It is normally the family of the bride which 'pays' with both gifts and money in order to find the most suitable possible bridegroom.

Death is the most impure event. It affects the entire group of relatives to varying degrees, but most of all the oldest son. It is he who is primarily responsible for carrying out the cremation ceremony, and the rituals that go with it. Years afterwards, a ritual must still be celebrated for the deceased on the anniversary of his death, and no significant event can be begun without commemorating one's ancestors.

Shiva and Parvati at a window of their temple, Kathmandu

FESTIVALS

Unlike Westerners, with their compulsive need for careful historical documentation and unbending addiction to proven fact, the majority of Nepalese unquestioningly accept and enjoy their festivals as 'something they have always done'. They love the rich assortment of folk-tales and earthy scriptural stories.

Here most of the festival celebrations originated centuries ago and have been carried down through the ages from some mythological or perhaps actual event, still re-enacted for reasons blurred by the passage of time. In Nepal, as in all other countries, festivals are celebrated in slightly different ways and with varying degrees of intensity, depending upon locality, economic and social status, education, religious and family background, and personal inclination.

For example, *Dasain* has different meanings for different people: some say that the festival lasts for ten days, hence it is called so; others believe that this festival removes ten kinds of sins of people; most others hold that it means Ram's victory over Ravan, symbolizing the victory of *truth* over *falsehood*; while some other Nepalis celebrate the festival in honour of the goddess Durga, praying that the goddess may bless them with a long and happy life.

Similarly, the *Holi* Hindu festival in March or late February, named allegedly after the mythical demoness Holika, has different meanings for different Nepalis: some connect the festival with the story of Prahalad, a true devotee of God, harassed by his own cruel father but saved by his kind sister Holika from a fire designed to burn him to death; others connect the festival with the activities of Lord Krishna; while most others see the festival as one creating the feelings of love and friendship amongst people by helping them forget the bitterness, enmity and hatred that they may have with one another.

During this rowdy, eight-day period, men, women and children – foreigners as well as Nepalese – may find themselves doused with sacred red powder and/or splashed with scarlet liquid. You will find *Holi* is a great festival of feasting, merry-making and rejoicing.

In Nepal, the five days of *Tihar* – the glorious harvest moon season – are celebrated in October or early November. *Tihar* literally means 'a row of lamps'. Lighting displays are traditional, but this festival is actually a succession of significant holidays celebrated for a number of reasons. *Tihar* brings the worship of Laxmi, Goddess of Wealth. Worshipped in turn are the lowly dog and ill-omened crow, as well as the sacred cow, the family money box and the brothers of every home.

In late April or early May *Buddha Jayanti Purnima*, the full moon of Lord Buddha's birth, is celebrated. Buddhists from countries around the world come to visit Lord Buddha's birthplace in Lumbini. On his birthday the focal point for Buddhist activities is the massive, white-domed stupa which crowns Swayambhunath hill and which is the largest, most sanctified of all Nepalese Buddhist shrines. On this day thousands of Buddhists, together with their Hindu brothers, pay homage to Lord Buddha's exalted name.

During the August-September period the sacred lunar month of Gunla is observed and celebrated. Gunla is as holy for the Buddhist population as Lent is for Christians, or Ramadan for Muslims, or the four months of Chaturmas for Hindus. Throughout these auspicious thirty days Buddhists devote themselves with great enthusiasm to fasting, doing penance, going on pilgrimages, and attending holy ceremonies, with a typically Nepalese climax of feasting, merry-making and rejoicing.

KRISHNASTMI

During the seventh day of the dark lunar fortnight in August or early September, the day preceding the midnight hour glorified by Lord Krishna's birth, called *Krishnastmi*, is celebrated. In Nepal the great Lord Krishna is one of the most adored of all deities. The stories of his miraculous birth, fabulous childhood, endless romances and many deeds of valour have sunk deep into the imaginations and hearts of the Nepalese people. As his is a promise of the ultimate triumph of good over the ever-present evil in the souls of men, so the day of his birth is acclaimed by the Nepalese throughout the land.

The visitor to Nepal can almost literally feel the presence of Lord Shiva in Kathmandu Valley. His spirit is everywhere, dwelling in the thousands of idols and monuments which glorify his holy name, and pervading the hearts, minds and lives of the Nepalese people. *Shiva Ratri*, the sacred night of Lord Shiva, falls on the fourteenth day of the waning moon in February, or in some years in early March. At Pashupatinath – one of the most sacrosanct of all Hindu shrines – many commence their twenty-four-hour fast before dawn on Shiva Rastri day, when the temple in Kathmandu is already crowded with hundreds and thousands of devotees. Around the valley, in the city and village courtyards and at crossroads, bonfires are built and family groups keep all-night vigil to glorify the Supreme Lord of Creation.

Thus, visitors to Nepal will find that the Nepalese both love and dread the festivals, which indeed fill their calendar. Similarly, they will also find that the musical traditions in Nepal are as numerous as the different ethnic groups in the country. Along with these, visitors will also note that the entire diversity of rituals and forms of worship found throughout the country are not a matter simply of a ritual mixture of religions, but rather an expression of the fact that there are many gods – and many paths to religious salvation.

5

Travel in Nepal

Taleju Mandir – first three-storey temple in Kathmandu

TRAVEL ROUTES TO NEPAL

As visitors to Nepal, you may well consider doing some travelling on your own. Eight international airlines fly to the capital Kathmandu, with over 65 flights weekly. In addition, Royal Nepal Airlines offers foreign charter flights at request. Choose your destination airport in Nepal according to your onward travel plans.

Visitors travelling by car have a number of optional access points over the Indian-Nepalese border crossings of (1) Gorakhpur/Sunauli (West); (2) Raxaul/Birganj (Central); (3) Siliguri/Kakarbhita (East); and (4) over the Tibetan border crossing Kodari. An international *carnet de passage* is mandatory for all vehicles. You can travel by train or bus from almost all the large cities of India to the border of Nepal.

Inside Nepal, the only railway connection exists between Jainagar and Janakpur. The old locomotive might be of interest to railway buffs. The domestic service of the Royal Nepal Airlines has regular flights to all the important population centres. Moreover, there are additional flights to several famous Nepalese tourist spots. Buses and cars are readily available and are the normal means of transportation. They are, however, not the safest vehicles on the road and should be selected with great care.

Besides taxis, group taxis and *tempos*, there are also other transport options. Bicycles and rickshaws are used for private city sight-seeing and shorter distances. The price should be negotiated before beginning the trip.

VISITORS IN ROYAL CITIES

Increasing numbers of people, including tourists, are now visiting Nepal, either in groups or individually. If you simply want to 'discover' Nepal, there are a number of key attractions you should consider.

Garuda figure in Durbar Square, Patan

You will find the royal cities in the Kathmandu Valley – i.e. Kathmandu, Patan and Bhaktapur – quite fascinating. Kathmandu, the central city, has a number of special attractions, for example, the Palace and the Durbar Square, Rani Pokhari, Tudikhel Square, Singha Durbar, Narayan Hiti Palace, Basantpur Plaza, Gaddi Baithak, the votive temples, the Buddhist monasteries and sanctuaries.

Pre-eminently a Buddhist city, Patan is especially known for its more than 150 monastery complexes. Patan's fascinating places include Durbar Square, Mangal Bazar, Palace Garden, Archaeological Museum, Sundar Chowk, Krishna Temple, and various other temples.

Bhaktapur, the third of Nepal's 'Royal Cities', offers one a rare glimpse into a very nearly intact city of the Middle Ages. The Nepalese-German Bhaktapur Development Project was an influential contributor to the preservation of Bhaktapur's historical character. Things are especially lively on Potters' Square, Durbar Square, Mul Chowk, Sundhoka, Bhaktapur Museum, Shiva Temple, Durga Temple, and numerous other temples.

SUMMITS AND LAKES

The small city of Pokhara has a completely different atmosphere from the capital city. Picturesque valleys, gently rolling chains of hills with terraced fields of rice, sub-tropical forests and the unique silhouette of the Himalayas are the greatest attractions of Pokhara. One of the most beautiful places on earth, Pokhara gives you different views of summits like Dhaulagiri, Anna-

Phewa Lake near Pokhara

purna, Macchapucchre (Fish Tail), Lamjung Himal, Manaslu and Himalchuli; and of beautiful lakes like Phewa, Begnas and Rupa.

PILGRIM TRAILS

By far the most well-known hiking routes in Nepal among trekking tourists are the Jomosom/Muktinath trail and the well-trodden path to the Annapurna Base Camp. The beautiful landscape and mountain scenery along the deepest valley on earth will take your breath away. There are now sufficient small lodges and hotels along both trekking routes to provide shelter and comfort.

JUMLA AND DOLPO

A trip to the Jumla and Dolpo districts of west Nepal is very worthwhile and will give you the feeling that you are being transported back into the Middle Ages of Nepal. Rara Lake, Danphe Pass, the Malla Stones, and Khatyar Valley are the main tourist attractions in this region. However, because of the isolated location of these regions, and also because of their high altitudes, your trip does require a lot of preparation.

HELAMBU AND LANGTANG

Helambu and Langtang are the two fantastic trekking areas located closest to the capital city. These regions stretch between the chain of hills forming the northern border of the Kathmandu Valley and the main range of the Himalayas – the national frontier with Tibet. The Laurebina Pass, the lake groupings of Gosainkund, Panch Pokhari, the Langtang Lirung and the Big White Peak, along with the beautiful kholas (streams) and the temples of these regions, are the main attractions here.

MOUNT EVEREST

To see Mt Everest at least once must be the dream of each and every visitor to Nepal. At 29,028 feet (8,848m) it is the highest mountain in the world. This experience is much more intense when you follow the beat of your own drummer and hike up to the area on your own; any organized excursion from Kathmandu cannot give you that feeling. The renowned Everest View Hotel at 12,360 feet (3,850m), enjoys the status of being the highest located hotel in the world and is now back in service again. Namche Bazar, Everest Base Camp, Chhukung Meadow, Island Peak, as well as small villages high in the mountains are all memorable sights.

A view of Everest from the Kala Patar

NEPAL'S FAR EAST

As a visitor, you can still discover a piece of the original Nepal in the remote east and the Kanchenjunga – the second highest mountain in Nepal and the third highest in the world. For this hiking trip, the point of departure is Taplejung. The trail leads over terraced fields onto a mountain saddle at 8,366 feet (2,550 metres). The steep climbs take you through Kanch Base Camp, Chainpur, and Jamlingtar to Makalu Base Camp at an altitude of 16,400 feet (5,000 metres) by making a rewarding seven-day-long tour. From the base camp there are fantastic views of the summits of Mount Everest, Lhotse, and the Makalu. It is also possible to go on a three to four-day-long Arun river-rafting trip, which must be organized from Kathmandu.

LUMBINI AND JANAKPUR

Travellers entering into Nepal from India through Bhairahwa should not fail to visit Lumbini, Buddha's birthplace. Buses make the trip regularly and even taxis can also be taken – some bargaining may be needed perhaps. Janakpur is in the southeast section of the Tarai. In mythical times Janakpur was the capital of the old Mithila Kingdom, the king of which was the holy Janak, the father of Sita. Here in the Rama Mandir and Janki Mandir of Janakpur, both Rama and Sita are worshipped as incarnations of the god Vishnu and his spouse Lakshmi.

Vivaha Panchmi in November/December is the most significant festival in Janakpur, commemorating the anniversary of the marriage of Sita and Rama. Thousands of pilgrims from different parts of Nepal and India, as well as from other countries come here during *Vivaha Panchmi*. Every year this festival is celebrated with great enthusiasm.

NATIONAL PARKS

Nepal is a paradise for bird lovers. Over 800 bird species have been observed here. In addition to the birds, Nepal can also offer a broad array of butterfly varieties. So far, over 600 varieties have already been registered, which include several of the rarest species on earth. The animal world of Nepal has always attracted the attention of visitors, adventurers and explorers.

At present there are 13 national protected areas, which comprise more than nine per cent of the total land area – one of the highest percentages in all of Asia. As a visitor, you can get the best insight into the fauna and flora of Nepal through a description of its national parks and wildlife reservations – e.g. the Royal Chitwan National Park, Sagarmatha National Park, Langtang National Park, Shey-Phoksumdo National Park, Rara National Park, Annapurna Conservation Area, The King Mahendra Tourist Park for Nature Conservation, Royal Bardia National Park, Suklapantha Wildlife Reserve, Koshi Tappu Wildlife Reserve, Shivapuri Reservation, and Khaptada National Park.

6

Business Etiquette

Carpet-knotting

Recent political changes in Nepal have led to rapid moves towards a market economy. The Nepalese government has embarked on a wide-ranging programme of privatizing and restructuring state industry. The reforms suggest that Nepal is moving forward.

Since 1990, hundreds of new businesses have been registered in Nepal. Foreign investors may operate in any branch of the economy either as a limited liability company or as a joint stock company. Banking facilities for such businesses are constantly being improved and a shake-up is also being implemented in foreign trade financing.

Nepal is keen to encourage foreign investment. But you would always be well advised to check the current legislation on conducting business, as the law is evolving alongside all the other restructuring processes that are taking place. If you are involved, or intend to get involved, in business in Nepal, you should study the recently reformed foreign investment laws of the country. Obtaining reliable Nepalese legal advice as well as professional translating and interpreting services is also likely to be important in any business context.

Obtaining a contract in Nepal may take a long time. The Nepalese are still suspicious of being short-changed, and they are very cautious about taking risks. A knowledge of the Nepalese languages, especially Nepali, an understanding of the Nepalese culture and mentality and a full-time presence in Nepal by members of the negotiating team will ensure that your efforts are not wasted. The main difficulty in finalizing a contract in Nepal is likely to be concerned with how the deal is to be financed and paid for.

Top Tip: Understanding 'Time' & 'Improvization'

It is especially worth remembering that time hardly means money in Nepal. For the average Nepali time is an abstract philosophical concept. You may still find that letters are left unanswered, decisions are delayed, opportunities missed, appointments postponed at the eleventh hour, people responsible are absent, or difficult to find. Nepalis are still best at improvizing and not at all bad when forced to meet deadlines.

Telecommunications in Nepal are developing, and the whole system is undergoing general modernization. After years of a centrally-run economy, Nepalis are now learning how to adopt new managerial skills, including decision-making and undertaking personal responsibility.

Coming to Nepal on business unprepared may be a waste of time. You would be well advised to take advantage of getting to know as much as you can in your particular field before you come. Talking to Nepalese expatriates living in your country, for example, or seeking information from academic sources known to you, approaching official Nepalese tourist authorities or diplomatic and commercial missions can all contribute to your 'data base' and also help build your self-confidence.

Standard hotels in Nepal are scarce and the prices for accommodation are therefore high. If you plan to travel to Nepal frequently, you might be better off renting a flat in Kathmandu and/or in any other Nepali town of your choice. With business privatization in Nepal this will not be difficult. Nepalese newspapers usually carry advertisements some of which are in English as well. Besides, there are also many recently-formed accommodation agencies ready to help.

Note that in the Nepali business world only the written word is legally binding. Business lunches are very much acceptable in Nepal and the better-class restaurants provide a crisp, but relaxed service. The person who is trying to secure a contract pays for the meal. During negotiations you are expected to be clear, consistent and precise; things have to be logical to be accepted. When drawing up contracts, the Nepali side will insist on precision; a verbal agreement is only a preliminary to a written agreement, which alone is legally binding. As long as written documents have not been signed and exchanged, you cannot be sure of having secured anything. Any written contracts and agreements need to be checked meticulously by both parties involved.

Do not forget to shake hands when meeting someone both at the beginning of the meeting and before leaving. If you are introduced to several people in the room, it is usual to shake hands with everyone present.

Dress carefully when visiting prospective clients or business contacts in Nepal. The way one dresses is seen as an expression of one's attitudes and opinions. Dress should be quite formal – suits and ties are best, although some Western businessmen do wear safari-suits, especially in hot weather.

The Nepalese people are unusually sensitive to criticism, especially from foreigners. Even so, you do not have to go out of your way to flatter just for the sake of it; good manners dictate you avoid criticism as much as possible.

Top Tip: Remember Christmas/New Year Greetings

Once you have returned from Nepal to your own country, it would be regarded as a nice gesture to remember your Nepalese contacts the following Christmas (or, preferably, New Year) by sending them small gifts, such as calendars.

Shopping/Food
Out & About

Souvenirs in Basantpur Square, Kathmandu

SHOPPING

If you have time, a shopping trip in Nepal could be very worthwhile. But remember, haggling and bargaining is a prerequisite. Although haggling over prices has now become rather obsolete in department and large stores, as well as in most modern shops where the price of goods is clearly marked, bargaining is still possible in the markets and covered bazaars of most Nepalese towns and cities where products do not carry price tags. Always remember that you are supposed to negotiate, not to fight, with the salesperson!

There may be no obvious connection between the worth of the goods offered and the price demanded. If you feel this is the case, then even if you offer half the quoted amount it still may be more than the fair price. To avoid this problem it is a good idea to wait until you get a feel for the going rates. At all times, do not be hurried by the vendor, do not be afraid of refusing to buy if you feel the price is still too high, and have a look at the produce of several sellers before buying anything.

Finished handicrafts are on sale everywhere. For example, you will find statues of deities made of brass and bronze, beautiful wood carvings, and religious pictures called *thangkas*. The jewellery of the Nepalese gold and silver smiths of Kathmandu and Patan is especially beautiful. Wonderful hand-woven textiles, batiks, cloth handbags, clothing, woollen blankets, and hand-knitted sweaters are available in a great variety of colours and designs.

Nowadays in Thamel and Durbar Marg you can find a variety of fashion boutiques offering top brand names. Hand-woven Tibetan woollen carpets are also available in all sizes and colours. Calendars, art prints, gift-wrapping papers, memo books, and postcards from hand-made ore silk are all very popular mementoes. In recent years, cassettes of Nepalese folk music have become much sought-after souvenirs.

FOOD & HOME

The staple diet in Nepal is boiled rice, usually eaten in the form of *dhal baat* (rice and lentils) supplemented with a wide variety of vegetables and various types of spicy chutney. In the higher mountainous areas where rice is not grown, barley or potatoes are the staples.

Being a Hindu kingdom, beef is forbidden of course, but goat, chicken, pork and even buffalo are available, although the cost limits these options to the very few. Essentially, therefore, most Nepalese remain vegetarian. In the Tarai region variations of various types of Indian food are available, such as chapatis. Elsewhere, there is Tibetan food, including dried yak meat and Sherpa dishes, including spiced potato pancakes (*qurr*).

The Nepalese eat with their fingers, but only ever using their right hand since the left hand is used in bodily functions and deemed unclean. Outside of restaurants which cater for Westerners, where a knife and fork are provided, a stranger might be offered a spoon. The cooking area in a Nepalese home is a very private place which a stranger should always respect. The open fire is also a sacred thing and should not be used to incinerate bits and pieces. Visitors to a private home should take their shoes off at the entrance to the premises.

The most popular forms of drink are the home-made brews (to be approached with great caution!) distilled from rice, potatoes and wheat. The best known commercially produced product is Khukri rum.

Incidentally, like much of the Indian sub-continent, gambling is commonplace in Nepal – the board game *bagh chal* (goats and tigers) which is a bit like draughts, is a typical example and is widely played. There are casinos in the top Kathmandu hotels.

TREKKING PERMITS

The trekking permits are issued in the immigration offices. They can only be applied for in Nepal. The process is executed in the same manner as with visas. If you plan to undertake two different trekking tours, you must also apply for two separate permits. Remember, if you have a trekking permit, a visa is not required. Procuring a trekking permit through one of the trekking agencies is usually time-saving and even cheaper. The permit must be taken with you during your hike and presented at checkposts along the trails.

ROUND TRIPS

The valleys of Kathmandu and Pokhara are the traditional sight-seeing areas for tourists. Almost all travel agencies organize sightseeing tours in the three royal cities of the Kathmandu Valley. In addition, several travel agencies specialize in particular regions and offer matching tour packages. There are round trips between three and fourteen days in length; these vary in their degrees of comfort.

ALCOHOL

The buying and selling of alcohol in Nepal requires no special permission. There are good domestic spirits. The Nepalese are not familiar with wine, although attempts are now being made at producing fruit wines with similar methods. Foreign alcoholic beverages, especially whiskey, are comparatively expensive here due to high import duties so they make welcome gifts.

CUSTOMS

International customs regulations apply in Nepal. Do not bring in or out any illegal drugs, weapons or radio equipment. Articles for personal use are allowed up to a specified limit. Sometimes value assessments are entered into passports upon entry; upon exiting these must be presented again.

Remember that antiques which are more than 100 years old cannot be taken out. In case

---

Top Tip: Beware of Local Dishes!

In the first few days you should avoid consuming the local food, since the various dishes are usually cooked with a lot of oil and are heavily spiced. You will find that most of the restaurants in the Kathmandu Valley and in Pokhara offer a variety of culinary delights. Besides Nepalese cuisine, you can have everything from Italian to Russian food.

you are not sure of such things, arrange for the Archaeology Department of Ram Shah Path (Kathmandu) to provide you with a certification.

GUIDES

In the Kathmandu Valley as well as in Pokhara there are numerous tourist guides who have a good knowledge of English or another foreign language. You can either arrange for a guide or join an organized tour through any of the many travel agencies. Fees per day are a matter of negotiation between the tourist, the travel agency and the guide.

PHOTOGRAPHY

Photography is allowed in most places in Nepal, except at military installations and some holy places. If you want to take individual photographs of any Nepalese, please ask the person/s concerned in a friendly way if this is possible. You can purchase films just about anywhere in Kathmandu and Pokhara, and also get the processing done at an acceptable standard. However, you are advised to have your slides developed at home.

TIPPING

Tipping is not necessary in most cases in Nepal. In general, tipping is not required at restaurants, tea houses, coffee houses, bars or barber shops. Nor do you have to tip taxi drivers either. However, there are some occasions when tipping is required. For example, you should tip the airport or station porter who carries your luggage. Hotel room-service waiters, errand-runners, hotel pages, carriers on trekking tours and maids receive tips for their good service.

GIFT-GIVING

In Nepal, given the naturally friendly nature of the Nepalese, exchanging gifts, chatting at public places, and making friends are extremely good ways to advance a sense of common well-being and thereby make your trip so much more worthwhile.

Gift-giving is almost a ritual in Nepal. Mostly town and city-dwellers exchange gifts on New Year's Day, on *Dasain* and *Tihar* festivals, as well as on such special occasions as birthdays, graduation and weddings. It is only rarely, when a gift smells like a bribe, that you should return it immediately. Otherwise, you cannot decline a gift once offered to you unless you intend to insult the giver.

Top Tip: How To Present a Gift

When presenting a gift, Nepalis have a tendency to belittle it, saying, 'This is just a small token of love, nothing very much, really.' Before accepting the gift, the receiver in turn is expected to show reluctance, saying, 'Well, there was no need'. Make sure that you do not snatch the gift as if you were expecting it, saying, 'Aha! Thanks a lot'.

Unlike the Western custom, it may well be impolite in Nepal to open a gift in the presence of the giver. But when urged to do so, you should unwrap it with a degree of self-restraint.

RESCUE HELICOPTER

If, God forbid, you become seriously ill or trapped during a trek, a rescue helicopter can be ordered from the next radio, telegraph or tele-phone station through your trekking agency or embassy. It is important that you have a surety voucher in Kathmandu which guarantees the assumption of the costs. For further information in this connection, you may contact: *Himalayan Rescue Association*, Thamel, Tel – 222906/418755.

Threshing in the autumn

Useful Words & Phrases in Nepali

Buddha's all-seeing eyes, Bodnath Stupa

Nepali is the official language and principal means of communication in the multi-lingual, multi-ethnic country of Nepal. It is the mother tongue of more than 50 per cent of the Nepalese population and around 80 per cent of Nepalese understand this language. The status of English in Nepal is that of a foreign language, and it is understood primarily in the Kathmandu Valley and other towns and cities of Nepal, as well as in isolated instances on trekking routes.

Nepali sentence and phrase structures show concord in verbs and some modifiers like adjectives, participles and possessives. The grammatical features that control concord are person, number and gender.

The Nepali pronominal system has first, second and third person as English does. However, there are multi-levels of the first person singular 'I', second person 'you', and third person 's/he'. These levels are related to a scale of politeness, or of *honorific registers*, which indicates the relative status of speaker and addressee, which in turn depends on a combination of factors including relative age, sex, rank, role, etc. There are four levels in this scale: low (L), middle (M), honorific (H), and high honorific (HH).

PERSONAL PRONOUNS

1st person:

ma	I
haami (1)	royal I
haami (2)	editorial I
haami (3)	egoist I
haami (4)	inclusive I and you

2nd person
  Least Honorific

1.	tã	you (L)
2.	tïmi	you (M)
3.	tapaaĩ	you (H)
	yahãã	you (H)
	hajur	sir; you (HH)
4.	sarkaar	Your Highness (HH)
	mausuph	Your Majesty (HH)

  Most Honorific

3rd person
  Least Honorific

1.	u, tyo, yo	s/he (L)
2.	uni, tini, yini	s/he (M)
3.	wahãã	s/he (H)
	hajur	sir; you (HH)
4.	sarkaar	Your Highness (HH)
	mausuph	Your Majesty (HH)

  Most Honorific

Concord (Agreement)

Gender concord, which is a feature of many related Indo-Aryan languages, survives marginally in Nepali. There are two genders – masculine and feminine – and they are defined in terms of natural gender. The distinction is limited to human beings, animals of interest (e.g. the cow) and deified natural phenomena (e.g. the sun, the moon, sacred rivers, etc.). Otherwise, nouns that denote things are treated as masculine in gender. Nepali has two numbers: singular and plural:

	u	s/he
	uniharu	they
Person:	u khaancha	he eats
	ma khaanchu	I eat
Number:	u khaancha	he eats
	u khaanche	she eats
	uniharu khaanchan	they (male/s and/or female/s) eat

Only modifiers which have a base form ending in
-a, -i, or -aa may show gender concord with
nouns:

Gender:	raamro maanche	a nice man
	raamri aaimaai	a nice woman
	raamraa	
	maancheharu	nice people
	saano ketaa	a small boy
	saano keti	a small girl
	eutaa ketaa	one boy
	euti keti	one girl
But:	dhani maanche	a rich man
	dhani aaimaai	a rich woman
	dhani maancheharu	rich people

VOCABULARY

afternoon	diunso
boiled rice/rice	bhaat/bhujaa
breakfast/	naasta
refreshment	
clean	saafaa
cold	chiso
come	aaunu

dirty	phohar
evening	saanjha/beluka
food	khaanaa
friend	saathi
go	jaanu
hello/goodbye	namaste
hot	taato
house	ghar
large/big	thulo
less/little	thorai/alikati
market	bazaar
medicine	aushadhi
milk	dudha
month	mahinaa
more/much	dherai
night	raati
no	hoina
please	kripayaa
price	mol/mulya
room	kothaa
salt	nun
shop	pasal/dokaan
small	saano
sugar	chini
tea	chiyaa
thanks/thank you	dhanyabaad
today	aaja
tomorrow	bholi

vegetables	**tarkaari/sabji**
water	**paani**
week	**haptaa/saataa**
year	**saal/barsha**
yes	**ho**
yesterday	**hijo**
yoghurt	**dahi**

PHRASES AND SENTENCES

thik cha	Okay
tapaainko naam ke ho	What is your name?
mero naam . . . ho	My name is . . .
mero ghar . . . ma ho	I live in . . .
kati taadhaa cha/ parcha	How far is . . .
ma kasari pugna sakchu	How do I get to . . .?
yasko kati parcha/ lagcha	How much does it cost?
tyo mahgo cha	That is expensive
malaai menu dinus	Could I have the menu please?
malaai paani dinus	Could I have water please?
malaai piune kuraa dinus	Could I have something to drink please?

bill dinus	The bill please
makaai sancho chaina	I don't feel well
tyo ke ho	What is that?
aile kati bajyo	What is the time now?

NUMBERS

ek	1	pachaas	50
dui	2	saathi	**60**
tin	3	sattar	70
chaar	4	assi	80
paanch	5	nabbe	90
chha	6	sai/eksai	100
saat	7	hazaar	1000
aath	8	das hazaar	10,000
nau	9	laakh	100,000
das	10		
bis	20		
tis	30		
chaalis	40		

Facts About Nepal

CLOTHING

If you are planning to tour this Himalayan Kingdom, your route and the time of your travel are decisive factors regarding the choice of clothing. Having said that, you should always be prepared for a sudden change in the weather, even in summer. So, take a sweater with you in summer as well. In winter a light and warm sweater/jacket is recommended. In the mountains, you need warm wool or down clothing as well as hiking shoes. Items such as warm wool and cotton clothing, sweaters, footwear, and so on can be obtained in Nepal, or you can hire them in special shops. The best places with the greatest selection of new and used expedition and mountaineering equipment you can find in the Tibetan shops of Thamel in Kathmandu.

Nepal's Climate

Given the wide difference in elevation, Nepal's climate is unsurprisingly varied. In the Tarai the conditions are subtropical monsoon, through a warm temperate climate between 4,000-7,000 feet, cool temperate between 7,000-11,000 feet, alpine climate between 14,000-16,000 feet. Above this, temperatures are always below freezing.

	Average Temp. Jan	Average Temp. Jun/July	Average Annual Rainfall
Kathmandu Valley	10C (50F)	26C (78F)	58 inch (?cm)
Pokhara	4C (40F)	38C (100F)	100 inch (?cm)

CURRENCY/MONEY EXCHANGE

The Nepalese national currency is the rupee (NR). As a visitor, you should exchange money only at banks or authorized agencies. Officially, only these places are permitted to handle foreign currency. Generally recognized credit cards and traveller's cheques are accepted at many hotels, restaurants and shops.

VISAS

Foreign tourists, except Indians for whom a visa is not needed, can stay in Nepal for a total of three months per year. Those with special reasons can under certain circumstances have their visas extended for another month. The Immigration Office belongs to the Ministry of the Interior, which makes these decisions. Foreigners who have entered with a tourist visa are not permitted to work in Nepal either for organizations or as individuals. The visa regulations are frequently changed. Find out about the most recent rules on your arrival in Nepal.

HEALTH PRECAUTIONS

There are no longer any obligatory vaccinations for Nepal. However, it is advisable to get immunized against cholera, typhus, tetanus, and hepatitis. In any case, check with your doctor/health service. Travellers to the Tarai interior should under certain circumstances take a prophylaxis against malaria. As you never know, so in your travel apothecary you should definitely pack the following medications: malaria tablets if required, drugs against nausea and diarrhoea, antibiotics, insect repellents (lotions), protectants, antiseptics, bandages and mineral tablets.

Hospitals

There are some very good hospitals in the Kathmandu Valley: e.g.

Kalimati Clinic: Tel - 270923
Bir Hospital: Kanti Path, Tel - 221988
EIWEC Clinic: Baluatar, Tel - 410983
Kanti Hospital: Maharajganj, Tel - 411550
Maternity Hospital: Thapathali, Tel - 213216
Teaching Hospital: Maharajganj, Tel - 412303
Teku Hospital: Teku, Tel - 211344
Patan Hospital: Lagankhel, Tel - 522278 and
Bhaktapur Hospital: Bhaktapur, Tel - 610798

NATIONAL SYMBOLS

The cow is Nepal's *national animal*, called *Gaaitrimaataa* (mother-cow). The Hindus believe that the five products of the cow – milk, sour milk (curd), butter, urine, and dung – have purifying properties. Once a year in the Kathmandu Valley, the *Gaijaatraa* festival – which extends over eight days – takes place in honour of the holy cow and to commemorate the dead.

The Himalayan pheasant, which the Nepalese call the *daanphey-chari*, is Nepal's national bird. The male *daanphey* is particularly conspicuous with its strikingly beautiful plumage and its long tail.

The red rhododendron which is called *laaligurans* in Nepal is the national flower of this country. It grows in the Himalayas at altitudes above 2,000 metres in real rhododendron forests.

Yeti, 'the abominable snow-man', has also become a national symbol of Nepal. In the face of numerous Yeti-guests, or even hunting expeditions, the Nepalese government was forced to set down laws forbidding its killing and declaring this creature (if it exists) to be the property of the people.

No one has ever counted all the temples, shrines, and statues of the Kathmandu Valley. This would perhaps be a futile exercise. In nearly every courtyard and in many squares one finds an idol, an inscription, or the sculpture of some ruler or rich donor. Many of these art objects are centuries old, and some are of incalculable value.

Lakshmi Prasad Devkota is generally considered as the most outstanding Nepali poet of the twentieth century, worthy of a place alongside the foremost literary figures of modern South Asia.

Nepali Words Used In This Book and Useful Religious Terms

arti 1
: religious worship in a temple (cf *puja* in monastery)

baag chal 59
: 'goats and tigers' board game

bhajan 1
: See *arti*

Buddha Jayanti Purnima 41
: full moon of Lord Buddha's birth

Dasain 40
: festival of many meanings

dhal baat 59
: rice and lentils

Garuda 46
: half bird, half man – bearer of Vishnu

Gunla 42
: period of fasting

Gurkha/Gorkha 15
: lit. 'protector of the cows'

gurr 59
: spiced potato pancake

Holi 40
: festival of rejoicing (with many meanings)

Hukmi Sashan 13
: command of the Shah Kings

khukuri 15
: Gurkha knife

Krishnastmi 42
: Celebration of Krishna's birth

Lakshmi 50
: Goddess of Good Fortune & Prosperity; companion of Vishnu (Her symbol is the lotus flower)

Lumbini 41
: Buddha's birthplace

milansar 25
: warm, friendly

namaste 35
: traditional form of greeting

Nepala Mahatmya 37
: ancient text

Parvati 39	companion of Shiva, daughter of the Himalayas
Pratinidhi Sahha 14	lower house of parliament
puja 12	religious worship in a monastery
Rama 50	King of Ayodhya, seventh avatare of Vishnu; hero of the Ramayana
Rastriya Sabha 14	upper house of parliament
sel roti 28	deep fried rice meal
Shiva 39	'the destroyer' in the Hindu pantheon
Shiva Ratri 43	Sacred night of Lord Shiva
Sita 50	daughter of King Janak
thangkas 12, 58	religious items such as statues and pictures
Tihar 40	'row of lamps'/harvest moon festival season
Vishnu 50	Supreme Hindu god and saviour
Vivaha Punchimi 30	Main festival in Janakpur in Nov/Dec (commemorating marriage of Sita and Rama)

Index